WEAPONS & WARFARE

BY

JOHN GUY

Early Weapons & Warfare

The need for fortification has been with us since humans have been on the planet. Initially, strong dwellings were needed only as protection against the elements or from wild animals, but as man became more civilised, and hence more territorial, so the need grew to protect himself against his fellow man. That need has been with us ever since and seems likely to remain so. In the same way the primitive weapons that had been devised purely for hunting came to have a dual purpose: they began to be used to injure and kill *people*. The ingenuity with which humans have devoted their skills to destroying their own kind is perhaps a sad reflection on our species. No other animal expends such energy in pursuit of killing.

BRONZE AGE SHIELDS

Tribal leaders in Bronze Age Europe (c.2000BC-c.600BC) decorated both their weapons and their armour to display their position in the community. This magnificent bronze shield dates from the 1st century AD and was discovered at Battersea, in London, preserved in the mud of the River Thames. Made from bronze and gold, and decorated with red glass studs (then a valuable material), the raised patterns were fashioned by hammering from the reverse side.

THE AGE OF METAL

Prior to c. 2500 BC most tools and weapons were fashioned from stone. Hammers and maces were made by simply lashing a shaped stone to a wooden handle, while sharp flints, shaped to a point, made ideal spear and arrow heads. At about that time, however, the technique of manufacturing metals from natural ores developed. This hard-edged, bronze dagger (made from pouring liquid tin and copper into a mould) revolutionised weapon design.

THE MACE

Along with the spear, the mace is one of the earliest weapons used by man. In prehistoric times clubs were probably fashioned from the thigh bones of animals, or from hard, knobbly wood. The mace is a direct derivative of the simple club. By medieval times it had been fashioned into a formidable weapon, with the rounded end made of flanged metal and often reinforced with studs or spikes to pierce metal armour and inflict horrific injuries.

HILLFORTS

From about 1000 BC a type of fortification known as hillforts began to appear in Britain. They remained in use throughout the Iron Age until the Roman occupation. They were large communal, defensive enclosures, more akin perhaps to townships than individual fortifications. They consisted usually of a large, levelled enclosure on top of a hill, surrounded by one or more massive earthen ramparts, usually surmounted by timber palisades or stone walls.

BROCHS & DUNS

From about 200 BC another type of fortification, known as brochs and duns, began to appear in Iron Age Britain, principally in Scotland. They were hollow stone towers, about 40-50ft. high, usually circular or D-shaped, with timber buildings arranged around a central courtyard. Unlike hillforts, which were communal defences, these towers were the fortified farmhouses of a single family or small group of people. The impressive example shown here is at Furness, in the Orkney Isles.

THE ORIENT

In the West, an important purpose of armour (other than to offer its wearer protection) was to impress onlookers with its finery and craftsmanship. By contrast, the primary objective of this horrific Japanese mask was to intimidate and terrify the enemy – an early form of psychological warfare.

THE BIBLE AS HISTORY

This picture shows Joshua (chosen by Moses to lead the Israelites) defeating the Ammonites at Jericho. It is typical of many Biblical stories, which can be viewed as a collection of early historical writings, giving valuable insights into pre-Christian society in the Middle East.

Warfare in the Ancient World

Although man has probably always made weapons and waged war against his fellow man, it was the introduction of metal that revolutionised warfare. Swords were not very effective when only flint was available for making a blade – the weapon would have been too fragile and too heavy. The first swords were made of copper but were too soft and could not hold an edge. They became more effective after the introduction of tin (about 2500 BC) to make bronze, a hard metal which retained its cutting edge and was relatively easy to make. Although the Bronze Age is commonly held to have given way to the Iron Age at about 600 BC, in reality there was considerable overlap. Bronze was manufactured for weapons well into the Iron Age and iron was smelted as early as c.3000 BC in Asia Minor. Iron only gradually superseded bronze as the favourite material of warfare.

THE ROMANS

The emergence of Rome as the dominant city-state in the classical world owed much to the ancient Greeks and the Etruscans, who came from Asia Minor (or perhaps the Orient), establishing a number of self-governing city-states in Italy. The Romans quickly established a well-trained and well-equipped army that became the most efficient military force then known. A typical Roman legionnaire was equipped with a helmet, an oblong shield, a short sword and breastplate armour comprised of overlapping metal plates laced together, a type favoured by oriental armourers.

THE GREEKS

The ancient Greek army was largely a civilian force, each soldier supplying his own equipment so that the richest civilians became the best-equipped and most powerful soldiers. A typical soldier (known as a hoplite) was equipped with a bronze helmet (such as this bronze Corinthian example shown left, of c.500 BC) and a circular shield. Some soldiers carried short, bronze swords, but the usual weapon was a spear. The favoured method of attack was a massed assault by spearsmen to push an enemy back.

CHARIOTS

Horse-drawn chariots seem to have originated in the Near East, in Canaan, about 3000 BC. When the Egyptians extended their empire north, into Asia Minor, they brought back chariots and developed them into fast, light-weight fighting platforms. Chariots usually carried two men (one to control the horses and one to fight) and were employed throughout the ancient world. The example shown here comes from Babylon.

THE SIEGE OF TROY

In about 1184 BC Helen, wife of Menelaus, King of Sparta, was captured by the Trojans (Troy was a city-state in what is now part of Turkey). Menelaus's brother, Agamemnon, King of Mycenae, united the Greeks and attacked the city of Troy, but after 10 years was unable to capture it. The Greeks built a huge wooden horse, supposedly as a gift to the Trojans, and departed. Soldiers, hidden inside the horse, secretly opened the city gates to let in the returning Greek army, who then destroyed the city.

'GREEK FIRE'

'Greek Fire' was an early form of incendiary device employed by the ancient Greeks and remained in use, in differing forms, until medieval times. It is made from a compound of naphtha, saltpetre and sulphur, contained within earthenware pots, which were then set on fire and hurled at the enemy by the use of catapults. Because of the ingredients used, the flames would burn in water and so became a favourite weapon to use against an enemy's ships.

THE HITTITES

The Hittites (or 'sons of Heth') were a war-like people who occupied a large territory in what is now part of modern-day eastern Turkey. Their lands bordered the Mitanni (now part of Arabia) and Egypt. The Hittites were the first people to smelt iron extensively (from about 3000 BC) and their use of strong iron swords was probably instrumental in extending their empire over much of the Middle East.

ARMOURED KNIGHTS

Throughout Europe the development of arms and armour followed much the same pattern and flourished with the development of the feudal system. As the feudal system of government subsided, so the methods of warfare changed and the need for armour declined. In the 11th century, armour consisted principally of a helmet and chain-mail tunic, made up of inter-connecting metal rings. Because knights (and all soldiers) were expected to supply their own weapons and armour as part of their feudal service, the more wealthy could afford elaborate suits of plate armour, as shown here. Armour became so heavy and ponderous by the end of the medieval period that it hampered fighting and gradually came to be used more for ceremonial occasions than in war.

TACTICAL SUPREMACY

Towards the end of the medieval period (from about the mid-14th century on) the tactics of warfare began to change. The emphasis shifted away from attacking and defending castles, once considered the most important of strategies, to open warfare in the field. By this time armies consisted mostly of paid soldiers and mercenaries rather that the untrained soldiers provided by the feudal system. At the Battle of Agincourt in 1415, during the 100 years' war with France, England won a resounding victory against the superior forces of France, by the tactical use of archers.

JAVANESE KRIS

This highly ornate sword, with its wavy blade, comes from Java and is typical of many Indonesian and south-east Asian swords. Known as a 'kris' its use was mainly ceremonial, though it was also used in combat. Decorated with gold, silver and ivory, the blade was usually made of iron, which was then treated with acid to create decorative patterns.

CHIVALRIC CODE

Its very strict chivalric code belied the often barbaric nature of medieval warfare. Battles would often be decided by negotiation rather than by fighting, or champions might be called upon to decide the outcome, each side selecting a single combatant, or group of knights, to fight on its behalf. If captured, knights were not usually killed, but held to ransom. Never the less injuries inflicted on the battle field were quite horrific, many dying from secondary infections rather than their wounds.

Medieval Weapons & Warfare

The period in history known as the Middle Ages, or medieval period, was for many parts of the world an era of great upheaval. In Europe particularly, great power struggles were waged between lords and kings in their thirst for land. Many of today's political boundaries were established in this time. Europe and Asia were dominated by the feudal system, or variations on it, in which kings ultimately owned all the land in their kingdom, which they let out to various lords. They in turn let out their land to sub-tenants, lesser barons or knights. The result was a virtually continuous struggle for power and supremacy between either the king and his barons, or between the barons as they jostled for position.

THE VIKINGS

Contrary to popular belief, the Vikings did not usually wear horned helmets, though some leaders may have worn them on ceremonial occasions. A typical Viking warrior wore a helmet, sometimes with terrifying face mask (such as the one shown here), a tunic of chain-mail (or leather) and a circular shield. His favourite weapons were an iron sword, battle axe, long spear or bow.

JAPANESE ARMOUR

The development of oriental arms and armour followed a completely different course from that in the West (or Occident). Japanese armour was intended to terrify and intimidate the enemy as much as to protect its wearer. The favoured form was a type known as scale armour, made by lacing together overlapping metal or leather plates, often lacquered. Helmets were fitted with wide, splayed neck guards.

LONGBOWS & CROSSBOWS

Although the longbow was the favoured weapon of attack in battle because it had a longer range and was faster to fire than the crossbow, the latter was favoured by castle defenders because it was more deadly at close range. The crossbow had to be pulled back (usually by a winding mechanism) and fired a bolt (about 1ft. long). Both weapons were preferred to early guns, which were dangerous and unreliable.

A longbow

A crossbow

An early Medieval cannon

The Age of the Gun

Probably no other single event has had so profound an effect upon the practices of warfare, or indeed society, than the invention of gunpowder and the subsequent development of guns. Weapons and warfare changed very little for much of man's history, relying almost solely on sharp-edged hand weapons. The development of firearms a mere 600 years ago, however, changed all that with a subsequent and dramatic increase in loss of life sustained during armed conflicts. Although the Chinese have usually been credited with the invention of gunpowder, some doubt has now been cast on this. There are several other claimants, including India, Arabia and Greece. Certainly, its full potential was not recognised until European scientists invented the gun, probably in the late 13th century.

THE DEVELOPMENT OF HAND GUNS

Early guns were unreliable and accidents were common. If too much powder was introduced or flaws appeared in their metal barrels, the guns were likely to explode. Artillery was a new and inexact science. The foremost problem was how to ignite the powder without the need to carry a lighted touch-paper.

MATCHLOCKS: The earliest forms of hand-guns were matchlocks. They were fired by simply pouring the powder through a hole in the barrel and igniting it with a lighted touch-paper.

WHEEL-LOCKS: Wheel-locks dispensed with the need for lighting the gunpowder. A wheel mechanism created a spark by striking against iron pyrites in the chamber and so igniting the gunpowder.

FLINTLOCKS: In the flint-lock, the cock contained a piece of flint that, when triggered, hit against the metal hammer, creating a spark. By simultaneously exposing the gunpowder chamber, the powder was ignited.

THE FIRST GUNS

No-one knows who actually invented the gun. All that can be said with certainty is that the first illustration of a gun can be dated to 1326. No explanation is given so we must assume that guns were already commonplace and had been around for some years before that. Early guns were vase-shaped, but after about 1350 the more familiar hollow-tube shape made of wrought iron (shown here) began to appear, mounted on wooded supports. Projectiles were usually arrows or stone balls.

GUNPOWDER

It used to be claimed that the Chinese invented gunpowder (about 1045) but some doubt has now been cast on the accuracy of this date. What seems more likely is that several researchers in both Europe and Asia were working on similar formulae simultaneously. Either way, the full potential of gunpowder was not realised until the late 12th/early 13th centuries, when the first guns appeared. Its early use in China had been confined to making fireworks or creating large explosions to frighten an enemy (as seen here).

FRIAR BACON

Roger Bacon (c.1214-92) was an English Franciscan Friar who was in many ways ahead of his time. A scholar and scientist, he was very conscious of the superstitious times in which he lived and wrote down the results of his experiments in code to avoid persecution. Whether or not Friar Bacon was carrying out his own independent research or studying books brought back from China is not clear. What is certain is that he was the first person to write down the formula (c.1250) so that gunpowder could be manufactured to a consistent standard.

THE END OF AN ERA

Although the development of firearms has often been credited with sounding the death knell of the medieval castle, this was not the case. Early guns were neither reliable nor powerful enough to have much effect on stout castle walls. By the time guns were capable of causing substantial damage to stone walls, the day of the medieval castle had already passed.

A number of castles were either built, or altered, to accommodate guns, usually small handguns. The most common method was to change the more traditional cross-shaped arrow loop (shown here) to one resembling a key-hole shape. The gun barrel was passed through the circular hole while the gunner used the slot as a sighting line.

The Development of Firearms

Following the initial discovery of gunpowder, it was some time before anyone had the idea of using the explosive power of the substance to propel an object and use it as a weapon of war. Early guns were fired by placing the powder and shot down the length of the barrel and ramming down hard. This method was known as muzzle loading. Accidents were common and the method was very time-consuming, particularly important when under fire in the heat of battle. It soon became obvious that it would be quicker and easier to load a gun from the breech, or firing end, but this would necessitate a second opening into the barrel that had somehow to be closed securely at the moment of fire to prevent mishaps.

ARMOUR PIERCING

World War II saw the rapid advance and development of tanks and multi-gun fighter planes. Gun sizes on tanks increased from 40mm at the beginning of the war to a powerful 88mm by the end of the conflict. Mounted on swivelling turrets, first developed for use of guns on warships, such tanks became incredibly versatile and could pierce 3 inches of armour plate at 1000 yards. The example shown here is an American Sherman tank.

BREECH-LOADING HANDGUNS

Although breech-loading cannon appeared probably as early as the 14th century, safe, breech-loading handguns were not successfully introduced until the early 18th century. The obvious dangers were the risk of burning or explosion in the face of the firer if the chamber was not properly sealed. The first breech-loading rifle appeared in 1812 but did not come into general service until 1848.

NEW LINES OF DEFENCE

The introduction of artillery had a profound effect upon the design of fortifications. To begin with guns were simply accommodated in medieval castles by adapting arrow loops for the purpose, but as guns became more reliable and powerful new types of defences had to be designed to accommodate the new, larger guns and to protect against the effects of cannon fire. Medieval castles, which were already in decline by the 15th century, presented too large a target for gunners. Forts built after about 1500 were low to the ground with massive earthen embankments behind the walls to lessen the impact of incoming fire. The old-style battlements were replaced with deeply splayed embrasures with circular or pointed bastions to deflect shot and give the guns maximum field of fire.

AUTOMATIC GUNS

The development of automatic guns became possible after the introduction of metal cartridges. The first machinegun, or rapid-firing gun, was patented by an American, Dr. Richard Gatling, in 1862. It employed several barrels that rotated in turn. In 1883 the design of machine guns was revolutionised by Hiram S. Maxim, another American. His single-barrelled gun utilised the recoil action, which was used to load, fire and eject simultaneously. The gun was cooled by a water jacket covering the barrel and was capable of firing up to 650 rounds a minute.

BOMBARDS

By the mid-15th century, gunmakers were beginning to perfect their art. They produced guns that were both more reliable and less likely to explode and also of a much larger size. They were usually cast in bronze or, more commonly, wrought iron, consisting of separate iron tubes, held together with iron hoops. The largest cannons were known as bombards and some reached huge proportions, up to 18ft. long (5.5m), 18tons/tonnes in weight with a calibre of 25ins. (63.5cm).

FIXED BAYONETS

Until the development of rapid firing and repeating guns, when an enemy approached too closely soldiers had to resort to old-fashioned hand-to-hand fighting. Often infantrymen, right up until the end of the 19th century, still carried swords and most had a bayonet, a kind of detachable spear-head, that could be fixed to the end of a rifle.

HOW THE WEST WAS WON

It has often been claimed that guns were responsible for white immigrants being able to over-run the native American Indians. While this is undoubtedly true, it is only part of the story, for what really 'won the West' was the development of automatic weapons, capable of firing several rounds of ammunition without re-loading. The first hand-operated revolver appeared in 1818 and in 1836 Samuel Colt patented a percussion revolver with an automatically revolving chamber.

Inspirational Leaders of the Past

Throughout history there have been a handful of leaders whose deeds and exploits set them apart from all others. Most were military generals who led their armies in the conquest of other lands. Included among these are Alexander the Great, who extended the Greek empire in the twilight years of that civilisation in the 4th century BC and laid the ground for the Roman empire that followed. Rulers such as Alexander and Julius Caesar were intent not just upon conquest but also on the spread of their civilisations. By contrast, the ruthless Mongolian leader Genghis Khan desired only power and exploitation. Other great leaders arose in trying to defend their homelands from invasion, as with Hannibal, the brilliant Carthaginian general, and Boudicca, the Celtic British queen, both of whom tried to halt the advances of the Roman empire.

ALEXANDER THE GREAT (356-323 BC)

Alexander the Great inherited his father's kingdom of Macedonia when just 20 years old. An inspired leader, he always led his army from the front of the battlefield. By 323 BC, when he died prematurely of fever, he had extended his rule, and the Greek empire, to Persia (now Iran), Egypt, Asia Minor and India.

GENGHIS KHAN (c.1162-1227)

In the 13th century, the Mongols established one of the largest empires ever known, extending over most of China, southern Russia, much of eastern Europe and Asia Minor (what we now term the Middle East). The empire was centred on Mongolia and its most powerful and ruthless ruler was Genghis Khan. He was a cruel man whose name roughly translates to 'ruler of all men'. He is believed to have been responsible for over 30 million deaths

GEORGE WASHINGTON (1732-99)

George Washington was born in Virginia and fought for the English in the French and Indian wars of 1754-63. An honest man of humble birth, his integrity is said to have inspired his fellow Americans. He spoke out against British rule and led the revolution for independence, becoming the first President of the newly-founded United States of America in 1787.

HANNIBAL (247-182 BC)

Rome's second attempt to invade Carthage, a city-state in North Africa, was thwarted by Hannibal (a brilliant young Carthaginian general) in the Second Punic War (218-202 BC). He marched his army, together with 40 African war elephants, around North Africa, crossed to Spain and then proceeded to cross the Alps into Italy and strike Rome from the north, where it least expected attack. He defeated the Romans at Cannae in 216 BC, but was eventually beaten in 202 BC.

THE DUKE OF WELLINGTON (1769-1852)

Arthur Wellesley, lst Duke of Wellington, was of Irish birth and began his distinguished career as a soldier. He quickly rose through the ranks, but is best remembered for defeating Napoleon Bonaparte at Waterloo in 1815. He returned home a hero and entered politics, becoming Prime Minister in 1828. He was the first leader also to be Commander-in-Chief of the British Army since Cromwell.

NAPOLEON I (1769-1821)

Napoleon Bonaparte was a French ruler and military leader of rare military genius with ideals of world domination, who is said to have inspired Hitler. War broke out between Britain and France in 1793 and resumed again in 1803, after a short truce. Napoleon won resounding victories in Italy (1796), Belgium (1797), Austria (1805), Prussia (1806) and Russia (1807). A charismatic man, he inspired his troops by looking after their well-being and ensuring they were well-fed. He was eventually defeated by a combined allied army and spent the remainder of his life in exile.

JULIUS CAESAR (c.100-44 BC)

Julius Caesar began his career in the Roman army and quickly rose to the rank of general. He also became a leading statesman in the Roman Senate. He conquered Gaul and invaded Britain (in 55 and 54 BC). He was later ordered by the senate to disband the army but invaded Italy instead. Rome had been a republic, ruled by elected statesmen, but Caesar became power-hungry and wanted to rule alone, as emperor. He became dictator from 49 BC on. It was feared that he was becoming too powerful which led to his assassination on 15th March 44 BC by his fellow politicians. He was deified after his death, later Roman emperors assuming the godhead and title Caesar in his honour.

Warfare Since the Middle Ages

THE ENGLISH CIVIL WAR

The English Civil War of 1642-49 was fought between Royalists (known as Cavaliers) and Parliamentarians (the Roundheads) and was the result of many years of conflict between the monarchy and parliament in deciding who should rule the country. In February 1645 Parliament created a revolutionary new military system, the New Model Army. Nationally organised and trained, and regularly paid, it dispensed with the need for mercenaries.

Although we nowadays often adopt the somewhat complacent view that bloody warfare belongs to the Middle Ages, the truth is that, not only has mankind never been free of war, but by far the worst conflicts have occurred in modern times, particularly in terms of casualties. Casualties in wars used to be confined mostly to those involved in the actual fighting, because of the hand-to-hand nature of the weapons used. The development of firearms and, more particularly, impersonal weapons such as bombs, however, which can inflict harm upon an enemy across great distances, has meant that civilian casualties are now very much a part of modern warfare, whereas before they were comparatively rare. Although it might sound absurd, in the past there was a kind of code of war. Today it is very much more impersonal with death and destruction inflicted by remote control.

CHANGING STRATEGIES

Before the full potential of the discovery of gunpowder was realised, with the development of firearms, its explosive properties were used to good effect in blasting the walls and gates of fortifications.

AMERICAN CIVIL WAR

The American Civil War was fought between eleven southern states (the Confederates) and the northern (Union) states between 1861-65. The resulting conflict was a particularly bloody encounter. A scorched-earth policy by the Unionists resulted in many Confederate families being made homeless. Civilian and military prisoners were crammed into 'concentration camps', where many died of disease. Short of men, money and supplies, the Confederacy was eventually forced to surrender.

CHARGE OF THE LIGHT BRIGADE

The infamous 'Charge of the Light Brigade', which took place during the Crimean War, fought between Britain and Russia in 1854-56, was one of Britain's worst military disasters. Confused orders and incompetent officers resulted in a lightly armed cavalry charge straight towards the massed Russian guns. Strategists were forced to rethink their methods of attack as a result of such catastrophes.

SAMURAI WARRIORS

Samurai warriors were an elite caste of bodyguards employed by noblemen in medieval Japan. They followed a very strict code and treated their swords with an almost religious reverence. It was said that, once drawn, their swords, which were two-handed with slightly curved blades, could not be sheathed again until they had drawn blood. The Japanese martial art of Kendo uses the traditional swords and face masks once used by Samurai warriors.

AERIAL ATTACK

Professor von Eberhardht developed the first effective anti-aircraft gun for the German armaments firm, Krupps, in 1916, by utilising the decreased air resistance in the upper atmosphere. It had a very long barrel and was capable of firing a shell a distance of over 60 miles.

Attack & Defence

The twin principles of attack and defence have always gone hand-in-hand. Every advance in new methods of attack was met by a corresponding advance in defensive techniques. History demonstrates this pendulum swing throughout the ages, where first one side gained the advantage only to be almost immediately outmanoeuvred by the other. Nowhere is this better illustrated than in medieval siege warfare, as the series of illustrations on these two pages show. While no expense was spared in the development of new military technology and weaponry, defences became ever-more impregnable. The ingenuity of the human mind seems somehow to excel when faced with the problems of attack and counter attack, perhaps inspired by the basic instinct of survival. Many of the most significant advances in science and technology first began as part of a military strategy. The most spectacular example of this in the modern world, perhaps, is the development of the rocket, from the 'flying bombs' made by German scientists during World War II.

THE GREAT WALL OF CHINA

The Great Wall of China is the only man-made feature on Earth that can be seen from outer space. It was ordered to be built by Emperor Shih Huang Ti in c.214 BC to keep out the Mongolian Huns to the north of China. Maintained and rebuilt several times since then, most of this massive construction, which runs for 2400 km/1500 miles, dates from the 15th - 16th centuries AD.

SIEGE TOWERS

There were many ways in which a fortress might be attacked. Archers could fire at defenders on the walls from behind wooden screens to give covering fire while others attempted to gain entry by scaling ladders or from the protection of a belfry. A belfry was a wooden tower that could be wheeled into position against the wall and then a drawbridge lowered from its top stage onto the wall top giving attackers direct access to the walls. However, ladders could be easily pushed away and belfries were susceptible to fire.

SIEGE ENGINES

There were a number of different siege engines to help attackers gain entry to a fortress, some so powerful that they remained in use long after the advent of guns. The mangonel (left) was a huge stone-throwing machine, similar to a catapult. Others were the ballista, a kind of giant crossbow, and the trebuchet, which resembled an enormous sling.

DEFENDING THE WALLS

Despite their bristling array of walls, towers and other defences, most castles were seldom called upon to withstand a siege. Their very presence acted as a deterrent and the outcome of confrontations was often decided by negotiation rather than by force. Sieges could last anything up to a year (or, exceptionally, longer) but were very costly. Most defenders surrendered when faced with disease or starvation.

JAPANESE CASTLES

Castles built in Japan and other oriental countries resemble, to western eyes, huge houses or temples and show few outward signs of being defensible. They were much stronger than they might first appear, however, with the living apartments ranged in tiers above a massive, featureless stone plinth that gave an attacker few opportunities to gain access. This view shows the 16th century Hiniesu Castle in Japan (Castle of the White Heron).

AGE-OLD METHODS

Methods of siege warfare changed little over the centuries and most of the siege engines described here were used by the Romans and even the ancient Greeks. Often the defenders inside a fortress also had their own siege engines to shower the attackers with stones or burning straw. They fired a variety of missiles, including stones, burning faggots, shrapnel or even dead horses to induce disease. Trebuchets could hurl a boulder weighing several hundredweight a distance of some hundreds of yards and could reduce a wall to rubble with concentrated fire.

SHRAPNEL BOMBS

The Chinese, although credited with its invention, were slow to realise the potential of gunpowder. Until the 15th century they confined its use to scaring away the enemy with loud explosions. They did, however, develop exploding shrapnel bombs, which they hurled among the enemy using traditional siege engines.

THE BATTLE OF JUTLAND

The Battle of Jutland was the only great sea battle of
World War I. It took place on 31 May 1916, off the
Danish coast between the British Grand Fleet,
consisting of 24 battleships, and the German navy.
Although the Germans claimed victory, they were
unable to force a way through the British fleet and
remained hemmed in for the remainder of the war.

THE FIRST
SEA BATTLE

Although ships had been a
feature of many battles,
the Battle of Sluys in
1340 is generally regarded
as being the first truly
naval battle. Edward III
defeated the French navy
during the 100 years'
war and established
English supremacy of the
Channel. There is some
evidence to suggest that
guns were mounted on board some of the ships, making
this the first use of firepower in a naval conflict.

UNDERWATER ATTACK

Prior to 1900 submarines were used mostly for
reconnaissance work, but afterwards, once fitted
with torpedo tubes, they became a very real
threat to shipping. The electrically-powered
Holland, shown here, was launched
in 1897 and three years later was
put into general service in
the U.S. navy.

Battles at Sea

*T*he control of seaways has always been an essential part of warfare but, for the most part, ships were used to transport men, equipment and supplies, and not as fighting vessels. There is some evidence to suggest that the Greeks and Romans may have mounted siege engines such as ballistas, large catapult-like machines, to hurl missiles or fire upon an enemy, but mostly ships were used as simple fighting platforms for soldiers. Even up to the 16th century, when cannon were mounted on ships, the guns were used to disable a ship so that the soldiers could overrun the crew; ships were expensive to build and it was considered better to capture and repair an enemy ship rather than sink it.

BATTLE OF TRAFALGAR

Admiral Horatio, Lord Nelson (1758-1805) won a decisive naval victory against the French at Cape Trafalgar in 1805, establishing Britain as the foremost naval power in Europe. British warships at that time could fire a broadside every 90 seconds, twice as fast as any of their opponents.

World War I (1914~18)

The underlying causes of the First World War were complex and, even now, are not entirely understood. At that time most of the major European countries were busy acquiring colonies around the world. The leaders of each country mistrusted the others and so a series of alliances were drawn up to achieve an even balance of power and prevent any one country from becoming too powerful. The spark that began the conflict occurred in 1914 when the heir to the Austrian throne, Archduke Franz Ferdinand, was assassinated. The Austrians blamed the Serbians and declared war on them. Russia went to Serbia's aid and Germany to Austria's. Germany had already been undergoing an armament programme and began to flex its muscles, initially to establish itself as the dominant power in Europe with little thought of an ongoing international conflict. However, when Germany invaded Belgium, which had been neutral until then, a threat was posed to Britain's maritime security and so Britain entered the war. Soon after, the conflict escalated into a world-wide conflict.

AMERICA ENTERS THE WAR

In the early stages of the war, German U-boats observed the international code of not sinking ships on sight, without warning. In February 1917 they ceased to do so, which threatened American shipping in the Atlantic. America had been supplying the allies and was forced to enter the conflict. Germany had hoped to defeat Britain before the U.S. could mobilise its strength, but seriously miscalculated events. Germany formally surrendered on 11 November 1918 and signed armistice agreements dictated by the allies.

GAS ATTACKS

When the war reached a stalemate position in the trenches, desperate measures were introduced to win the upper hand, including showering the enemy with poisonous gas canisters, such as mustard gas, which was a powerful irritant and caused severe burning. Soldiers had to wear cumbersome respirator masks as protection. Many died or suffered life-long respiratory problems as a result of even brief exposure to such gases.

CIVILIAN ARMY

The allied army consisted largely of untrained civilians and was initially no match for the German army. Britain, like other countries in Europe, had become complacent, and was unprepared when war was declared. Rising unemployment throughout Europe, however, meant that there was no shortage of volunteers, but there were serious shortages of materials, especially munitions. Women were forced to work in factories, shipyards and even the armed services to help with the war effort, in all the allied countries.

AERIAL WARFARE

World War I saw the first successful use of prolonged aerial attack in an armed conflict. Machine guns were mounted above the cockpits and bombs were dropped over the side, taking the fight beyond the range of land-based or ship-based guns. Aeroplanes were also used to spy on enemy positions.

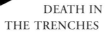

DEATH IN THE TRENCHES

Following the military deadlock after the Battle of the Somme, both sides dug themselves into trenches. Life in the trenches was inhospitable, wet and cold, and caused the war to drag on far longer than the six weeks most had expected the conflict to last. Complicated tunnels and dugouts were constructed with each side periodically going 'over the top' to attack the enemy lines under constant fire. Loss of life was horrendously high for very little strategic gain and many of those who survived suffered ill-health for the remainder of their lives.

MASS DESTRUCTION

For the first time in history, during World War I, the mass destruction of entire communities became possible, largely as a result of the massive new guns then being manufactured. Heavy guns, with a range of up to 60 miles, could bombard towns from a safe distance. Despite this, the basic tactics of the generals in World War I were the same as they had always been, in ranging armies in front of each other. The power of the weapons used, however, resulted in much higher casualty figures. Over 10 million people lost their lives in the conflict.

TANK WARFARE

Armoured cars had been used since at least 1904. But, the idea of completely encasing guns in heavily-armoured vehicles driven on caterpillar treads and able to traverse any terrain, was developed by a British Royal Engineer, Lt. Colonel Ernest Swinton. They were first used on the Somme in 1916 and then at the Battle of Cambrai the following year.

World War II (1939~45)

If the reasons surrounding the outbreak of World War I were complex and are, even now, unclear, the reasons for the outbreak of the Second World War are much easier to explain and grew directly out of unresolved issues at the end of the first world conflict. From a military point of view, many lessons had been learned from the first world war. In that war enemy troops still lined up in front of one another, in the time-honoured tradition, to 'shoot it out'. Battles in World War II were much more tactical and relied heavily on the increased use of technology and weapons of mass destruction. The war has been the bloodiest conflict in history thus far.

Altogether, some 40 million people lost their lives, including many civilians and 6 million Jews who were persecuted by the Germans and deliberately put to death in 'concentration camps'.

THE BLITZ

Having failed to defeat the British Air Force, Hitler continued his invasion plans by subjecting Britain to nightly bombing raids, both to destroy strategic targets and demoralise the civilian population. London was particularly badly hit as were other city centres throughout the world, including Dresden in Germany, bombed by the Allies.

GENERAL ROMMEL (1891-1944)

General Erwin Rommel was one of Hitler's leading generals in the early part of the war commanding Germany's highly successful tank corps. His defeat at El Alamein in north Africa, in 1942, is generally considered to be a turning point in the war.

AMERICA JOINS THE WAR

Japan joined forces with Germany and Italy, extending the war to much of Asia. Initially, America helped supply the allies against the Germans but was drawn directly into the conflict on 7 December 1941 when the Japanese launched an unprovoked attack on the U.S. fleet at Pearl Harbour, in Hawaii.

SUICIDE MISSIONS

Japanese soldiers had a reputation for fanaticism and would lay down their lives for their emperor rather than surrender or be shot. The 'kamikaze' pilots shown here were specially trained for suicide missions, to crash their planes, loaded with explosives, into the heart of the enemy. The word kamikaze means 'divine wind'.

D-DAY LANDINGS

The allies began their decisive push back against the Germans on 6 June 1944 with the re-invasion of France along the Normandy coast, known as 'Operation Overlord'. The Channel coast had been made impregnable by the Germans with a chain of fortifications. A British invention called 'Mulberries', or floating harbours, made the invasion possible. All told, some 5,000 ships transported over 300,000 men, 54,000 vehicles and 100,000 tons of supplies across the Channel, protected overhead by some 10,000 aeroplanes. Within a year the war in Europe was over (8 May 1945), followed 3 months later by the end of hostilities in south-east Asia.

BATTLE OF BRITAIN

In July 1940, shortly after France had fallen to the Germans, Hitler launched 'Operation Sealion', the code-name for his intended invasion of Britain. For the invasion to succeed, however, Hitler needed to establish air supremacy, so he threw the full might of the German airforce, the Luftwaffe, against Britain. For over 2 months an aerial battle (the Battle of Britain) was fought out in the skies above south-east England. It was the first major battle in history to be fought solely in the air. Losses were heavy, but the British Spitfires and Hurricanes eventually won the day over the German Messerschmitt 109s (shown left), preventing the invasion.

Inspirational Leaders of the 20th Century

MAO TSE-TUNG (1893-1976)

Mao Tse-Tung was a revolutionary Chinese leader and founder of the Chinese Communist Party (1921). When the Communists broke from the Chinese Nationalists in 1927, civil war broke out. He inspired an almost fanatical zeal among his followers and initiated a cultural revolution, making promises of social equality. He was Chairman of the Chinese Communist Party between 1949-76.

Whereas many of the inspirational leaders of the past have led their country to victory during campaigns of aggression, many of the greatest leaders of modern times have come to prominence more for their inspired resistance to aggressors, answering their nation's call during its hour of greatest need. A notable exception, perhaps, was Adolf Hitler (1889-1945) who certainly received fanatical devotion from his followers. However, the scale of atrocities during World War II prevents us from calling him an 'inspired' leader when the memories and consequences of that conflict are still too close in time to judge objectively. Future historians, with the benefit of the longer view, may judge him differently.

EISENHOWER (1890-1969)

Dwight David Eisenhower ('Ike') was a distinguished general in World War II, who afterwards went on to become the 34th U.S. President in 1952. He was the Supreme Commander of the Allied Forces in the 1944 invasion of Europe and also of N.A.T.O. forces in Europe after the war. He developed a personal approach to leadership that made him seem less remote to his troops.

SIR WINSTON CHURCHILL (1874-1965)

Considered by many to be one of the world's greatest wartime leaders, Winston Churchill (shown far left) succeeded in uniting the people of Britain and boosting morale when all seemed lost during the early years of World War II. A great orator, his rousing radio speeches lifted the spirits of an all but defeated nation. He became a Conservative M.P. in 1900, joined the Liberals in 1904 and reverted to the Tories in 1929. He became Prime Minister of a coalition government in Britain during the Second World War. In 1963 he was granted honorary U.S. citizenship.

GANDHI (1869-1948)

Not all great leaders came from a military background. Some like Mohandas Karamchand ('Mahatma') Gandhi, preferred a more peaceful resolution to human rights problems. An Indian nationalist leader, Gandhi spent 21 years campaigning for equal rights for Indians in South Africa. He advocated a policy of non-violent civil disobedience against British rule in India which, from a military perspective, was difficult to contain. He was a leading figure in securing India's eventual independence in 1947.

NELSON MANDELA (b.1918)

Nelson Mandela joined the African National Congress in 1944, so beginning his career as a black nationalist leader. He campaigned avidly for a free, multi-racial and democratic society in South Africa. Imprisoned between 1964-90 he became a political martyr, continuing to inspire the cause from his prison cell. He was eventually released following world-wide opposition to his imprisonment and was elected the first black president of South Africa in 1994.

'STORMING NORMAN'

The U.S. General Norman Schwarzkopf (nicknamed 'Storming Norman') led the allied attack on Iraq in the Gulf War of 1990-91. In August 1990 Saddam Hussein, dictator of Iraq, invaded neighbouring Kuwait when talks about oil quotas broke down. The United Nations imposed sanctions on Iraq followed by a short high-tech war, which was all over by April 1991. Schwarzkopf's raid on Iraq, in the final stages of the war, is said to have been inspired by Hannibal's attack on Rome (see pages 12-13).

GENERAL PATTON
(1885-1945)

Like other great U.S. leaders, General George Smith Patton believed that personal contact with his troops was essential for good morale. His most noteworthy campaign was in 1944-45, when he led the 7th Army across France and Germany following the D-Day landings.

STAR WARS

Both American and Russian satellite technology was based on the enormous advances in rocketry made by German scientists during World War II, when the V2 rocket was developed. The first communications satellite, 'Sputnik I', was successfully put into orbit by the Russians in 1957. Today, our skies are littered with several hundred communications satellites to aid the spread of information technology via computers, an essential part of modern missile warfare. The Strategic Defensive Initiative ('Star Wars') was a proposed system of orbiting space stations to detect and launch guided missiles.

AERIAL RECONNAISSANCE

One of the earliest uses to which both cameras and aeroplanes were put was to take aerial photographs of enemy positions. Developed during World War I, by the time of the Second World War a whole branch of the military secret service was engaged on interpreting the details of aerial photographs to follow troop movements and pinpoint bombing targets.

ELITE FORCE

Throughout history elite specialist forces have been employed to carry out specific missions, mostly in secret, and often used during peace-time when a government might not want to be linked to certain sensitive operations. Britain's Special Air Services (the S.A.S.) is generally regarded as one of the finest and most effective of these. Training is rigorous and only those capable of survival in the toughest conditions are selected.

THE U.S. MARINES

Only the best and toughest troops are selected for the U.S. Marine Corps. Personnel are trained in multi-skills, including air, sea and land tactics, and are capable of survival when dropped behind enemy lines. They are often the expeditionary force sent in to first engage an enemy and clear the way for the main military thrust to follow and as such usually face the fiercest opposition.

Special Forces & Espionage

Armies have always used spies to gain advance notice of an enemy's plans. Espionage was a particular feature of the 'Cold War' between the West and Russia, when both sides rearmed after World War II, and continues to flourish in today's world of sophisticated information technology. One of the most effective methods of secret warfare is for a small group of patriotic individuals to adopt guerrilla tactics against an enemy. The Boers used it against Britain in 1899-1902 and the Japanese during World War II. Its most effective employment in modern times, however, was probably by the North Vietnamese against the Americans, who were forced to adopt a strategy of defoliating the jungle to remove the guerrillas' cover.

ATTACK BY REMOTE CONTROL

A whole range of cruise missiles now exists, including the nuclear-armed Tomahawk, which can be launched from the ground, or from aircraft, submarines or warships, and directed by sophisticated computers to their targets. The Patriot missile (shown left) is a highly advanced mobile battlefield SAM (Surface-to-Air-Missile) system. It uses phased array radar for accurate target detection at several hundred kilometres and employs anti-jamming devices.

GUERRILLA WARFARE

When faced with the superior forces of a more powerful enemy, the smaller military forces of a patriotic or revolutionary movement often resort to guerrilla tactics. By dividing and isolating the enemy and making lightning strikes when least expected, such fighters can often create stalemate situations or even defeat a superior enemy. Guerrilla movements also usually have the added advantage of being able to mobilise the local population against the common enemy and being able to conceal themselves amongst them. From such a vantage point they can strike right at the heart of an enemy with sudden acts of harassment or terrorism.

EARLY WARNING SYSTEMS

The first advance warning system to detect approaching aircraft was Radar (Radio Detection And Ranging). It was invented in 1935 by Robert Watson-Watt and worked by transmitting radio waves and then scanning the returning echoes to measure the distance and position of the reflecting object. It was fitted to the Boeing B-17 'Flying Fortress' bomber, making it the first 'self defending' aeroplane. The system has been greatly advanced since then. The jet shown here has been specially adapted to carry an AWACS system (Airborne Warning And Control System). It carries long-range surveillance and detection radar with C3 (Command, Communication and Control) facilities to detect friendly aircraft, in addition to several other sophisticated tracking devices.

Attack from the Air

AIRSHIPS

Airships (known as Zeppelins after their designer, Ferdinand Graf Zeppelin) were huge, gas-filled dirigibles, but with a fuselage structure beneath the skin. They were cigar-shaped, with tail fins and an engine mounted in a cockpit suspended beneath, making them surprisingly manoeuvrable. First invented in 1900 they were used during World War I by dropping bombs over the side.

A new form of attack emerged during World War I: attack from the air, which has since become a major feature of modern warfare. From an early date guns were mounted on the flimsy new biplanes, but bombs were also dropped over the side of the cockpit. More commonly, however, bombs were dropped from huge airships, protected by fighter planes. Since the Second World War, aerial tactics have mostly been in the form of massed bombing raids (or, in modern times, the use of 'Smart' bombs which can pinpoint a target more accurately) to destroy strategic targets and significantly reduce an enemy's fire power before sending in ground troops.

STEALTH

'Stealth' is the popular name given to the technologies that enable aircraft, missiles or ships to avoid detection, either visually or by radar, sonar or infra-red sensors, thus making them virtually undetectable. Most commonly associated with aircraft, the Lockheed F-117A 'Nighthawk' Stealth fighter and the Stealth bomber (shown above) make an unforgettable sight, with their sleek black lines almost invisible to the human eye, even at close quarters.

FIGHTER ACES

Before interrupter gear was developed, which enabled fighter pilots to fire through the blades of the propeller, many biplanes in World War I had a machine gun mounted above the propeller, which made it difficult to aim. Nevertheless, the war saw several fighter aces, including the Frenchman Georges-Marie Guyneimer (shown here) who claimed 53 German planes.

BOMBS AWAY

Before the advent of rockets and guided missiles, the dropping of bombs from aircraft was very much a hit-or-miss affair. It was difficult to be accurate and pin-point a specific target from great heights. One solution was to employ massed bombing raids to obliterate an area, so increasing the chances of hitting a strategic target. When the allies began their daring daylight raids on Germany in the closing stages of World War II, the Americans lost an incredible 4750 B-17 bombers.

JET FIGHTERS

The jet engine was developed in Britain from 1937 by Frank Whittle. Although not used extensively in World War II, both Britain (with the Gloster Meteor) and Germany (with the Messerschmitt Me 262) had jet fighters in service by 1944. The first jet-to-jet combat took place in 1950 when the U.S. Lockheed F-80C 'Shooting Star' shot down a Soviet-built MiG 15 during the Korean War. The high-speed jets shown here are U.S. F-15C 'Eagles'.

HELICOPTERS

Although the principle has been understood since 1907, the first helicopter, with a powered rotor, the R-4, was developed by Igor Sikorsky (a Russian-American) in 1939. The first use of a helicopter used for troop transportation in combat was in 1951, by the U.S. 1st Marines during the Korean War. Helicopters have an obvious advantage over fighter planes in being able to take off and land vertically in difficult terrain, and in their greater manoeuvrability. Attack helicopters are mostly used to launch missiles, such as the McDonnell-Douglas 530 MG Defender, shown here, with missile launchers located either side of the fuselage.

SUPERIOR MACHINES

The main fighter plane used by Germany at the time of the Battle of Britain was the Messerschmitt 109, which was equipped with a central cannon. The British Spitfires and Hurricanes were equipped (at that time) with eight Browning machine guns, mounted in the wings (so interrupter gear was unnecessary) capable of delivering 9600 rounds a minute. This, coupled with their greater manoeuvrability, gave the British planes an obvious advantage over those of the Germans.

Modern Weapons & Warfare

KOREAN WAR

In 1910 Korea was annexed by Japan. When Japan surrendered at the end of World War II Russian troops occupied North Korea and American troops occupied the south of the country. In 1950 the Communist North Koreans, backed by the Soviets, invaded South Korea, which was aided by America and Britain, resulting in civil war. Open hostilities ended in 1953, but all attempts to unite the two factions have failed and they remain separate countries.

Since the end of hostilities in the Second World War there have been well over 100 major conflicts in some 70 countries world-wide. Many of these have been localised disputes, in under developed regions of the world, but several have been potentially inflammatory and may have led to further world-wide conflicts and have had to be quickly resolved. Following the end of the Second World War an arms race began between America (and her allies) and the Soviet Union. Each side acquired sufficient nuclear weapons to destroy the world several times over. Arms agreements were eventually reached in the 1980s and 90s and many warheads were disarmed, but since then several other countries have acquired weapons of mass destruction putting the world under constant threat of nuclear attack. Another feature of modern warfare has been the development of germ-warfare, where warheads containing lethal cocktails of bacteria are released on an unsuspecting civilian population.

GUIDED MISSILES

The idea of exploding rockets was first used by the Chinese as early as 1232. The first guided missile was launched in 1917, an automatically piloted biplane called 'Bug' SSM. During World War II, German scientists perfected the V1 and V2 pilotless 'flying bombs'. Once launched, the engines were timed to run for a set period of time, before they fell and exploded on impact. Modern computer technology means that missiles can select a target with pin-point accuracy.

GULF WAR

On 2 August 1990 Saddam Hussein, President of Iraq, invaded neighbouring Kuwait in a dispute over oil prices. The United Nations imposed economic sanctions on Iraq and on 29 November issued a resolution authorising the use of military force to liberate Kuwait. Hussein had been stockpiling weapons and many feared a long, protracted war, but what followed was a brief, high-technology war resulting in an allied victory, headed by America and Britain. The war began with a series of massive air strikes to limit the effectiveness of Iraq's ground forces, using several guided missiles that had never been tested in armed conflict before.

A NEW FORCE

Modern military forces are better equipped with weapons of destruction than any of their predecessors. Weapons of devastating capability can be launched from vast distances. Although 'Smart' weapons can avoid hitting unnecessary targets, modern neutron bombs are now capable of emitting short-wave radiation that affect people but leave buildings still standing.

ATOMIC POWER

The scientists who developed the atomic bombs that were dropped on Japan, so bringing World War II to a close, were Germans who had fled the Nazi regime and found sanctuary in America. The first generation of atom bombs used a combination of conventional explosives to drive together elements of Uranium 235 to produce a chain reaction among the neutrons. From these developed hydrogen bombs, which were more powerful than atomic bombs. Nowadays, a whole range of devastatingly powerful nuclear weapons is available to add to the armouries of military powers. When Japan continued to fight, even after the surrender of Germany, drastic action was necessary. It was decided to drop two atomic bombs on Japanese cities, Hiroshima and Nagasaki (bottom right). So devastating were they that both cities were virtually razed to the ground and people still suffer the effects of radiation. Japan surrendered almost immediately, on 14 August 1939. The picture above shows a nuclear bomb test in the Bikini Atoll (in the Pacific) in 1954, with the typical mushroom-shaped cloud.

VIETNAM WAR

Civil war broke out in Vietnam in 1954 between the Communist - backed north and the American-backed south. The north used guerrilla warfare, using the jungle as a refuge. The Americans responded with a scorched-earth policy of deforestation, but it proved ineffective. American troops were gradually withdrawn between 1969-73 in response to public pressure. Two years later South Vietnam surrendered to communist rule.

DID YOU KNOW?

That croissants were invented to commemorate a siege? Although usually thought of as French, croissants were first made by Austrian bakers. In 1683 the Turks laid siege to Vienna and began tunnelling beneath the city walls. Bakers, working through the night to make bread, heard the tunnellers and raised the alarm, thus saving the city. Viennese bakers devised the croissant (based on the crescent moon symbol on the Turkish flag) to commemorate the event.

That Navajo Indians speak a secret language? During World War II Navajo Indians were employed by the American government to pass secret military messages in code using their native tongue. The unwritten Navajo language is practically indecipherable to anyone who does not speak it and it was used as the basis for a cryptic code that neither the Germans nor the Japanese were ever able to crack.

That rockets provided the first air mail service? Although more commonly associated with warfare and, in modern times, space travel, early rocket pioneers experimented with many other uses to which this invention might be put. In 1928 the Austrian engineer Friedrich Schmiedl experimented with rockets that had hollow nose cones, containing mail, that separated in flight at a prescribed distance and parachuted to Earth. The experiments were continued in Scotland in the 1930s by Gerhard Zucker to deliver air-mail to the islands. Despite some success, the experiments were abandoned.

How French cuisine came about? French cuisine is today famed the world over for its variety and creativeness, but did you know it first came about as a result of a siege? In 1870-71 the Prussians laid siege to Paris, cutting off all its food supplies. People were forced to eat horses, cats, dogs, frogs, rats and even animals from the zoo in order to survive. To disguise the taste, cooks devised all manner of unusual sauces and recipes to make the food palatable.

That bombs can bounce? During World War II it became necessary to destroy strategic dams in Germany. The British inventor Barnes Wallis devised bouncing bombs that would skim across the water like flat stones until they hit the dam wall, whereupon they sank to the required depth and exploded. The shock waves collapsed the dams.

That Hitler was a secret believer in the occult? In the Hofburg Museum in Vienna is a spear, called the Longinus Spear after a Roman centurion who owned it, that is reputed to be one of those that pierced Christ's side as he hung on the cross. The spear assumed occult significance as a lucky talisman and was said to bring victory to anyone who owned it. Past owners included Constantine the Great and the Emperor Charlmagne. Hitler, who was very interested in the occult, acquired it and had it placed in a vault at Nuremberg Castle. Shortly after its discovery by American troops in 1945, Hitler is supposed to have committed suicide.

ACKNOWLEDGEMENTS

We would like to thank: Graham Rich and Peter Done, for their assistance.
Picture research by Image select. Printed in Italy. Copyright © 1998 ticktock Publishing Ltd, U.K.
First published in U.K. by ticktock Publishing Ltd., U.K. All rights reserved.
No part of this publication may be reproduced, stored in a retrieval system, or transmitted in any form or by any means, electronic, mechanical, photocopying, recording or otherwise, without prior written permission of the copyright owner.
A CIP Catalogue for this book is available from the British Library. ISBN 1 86007 031 0

Picture Credits: t=top, b=bottom, c=centre, l=left, r=right
AFP/Corbis-Bettman; 30l. AKG; 2br, 5cr, 12/13cb, OFC & 13cr, 13t, 12cb, 15tl, OBC & 17bl, 17tl, 16tl, 18/19, 22bl, 23tr, 24/25c, 25c, 25br, 24bl, 27br, 26c, 29tl, 30bl, 28tl, 31br, 31tr. Ancient Art & Architecture; 2/3c, 2tl, 3tr, OBC & 5tl, 5br, 6bl, OFC & 6/7c, 6tl, OBC & 6c, 8/9cb, 13br, 17tr. Ann Ronan @ Image Select; 3br, 2bl, 5tr, 4/5c, 4/5cb, 7br, OBC & 9tr, 8bl, 11tr, 10/11cb, 10cl, 10bl, 11tl, 14br, 14bl , 16bl, 16br, 18c, 28bl. Chris Fairclough/Image Select; OFC & 10tl, 14tl, 28/29b. Corbis-Bettman; OBC & 4l, OBC & 15r, 26br, 31br, 32c. et archive; 18tr, 18tl. Courtesy of Fine Art Photographic Library; 15c. Giraudon (Paris); IFC/1, 2/3cb, 17br, 20bl, 21r, 20tl, 21br(x2). Hulton Getty; OBC & 23b, 22b. Image Select; OFC & 7tr, 9br, 11br, 12tl, 12/13cb, 21t, 20br, 22tl, 23l, 24tl, 25tr, 29br, 31c, 30/31cb. Mary Evans; 8/9ct. Pix; 24bl. Quadrant Picture Library; 27tr, 29t. Rex Features London; 26r, OFC & 26tl, OFC & 28/29c, 30/31ct. Sipa Press (Paris); 27l. l.

Every effort has been made to trace the copyright holders and we apologise in advance for any unintentional omissions.
We would be pleased to insert the appropriate acknowledgement in any subsequent edition of this publication.

snapping-turtle
guide